this book belongs to

____

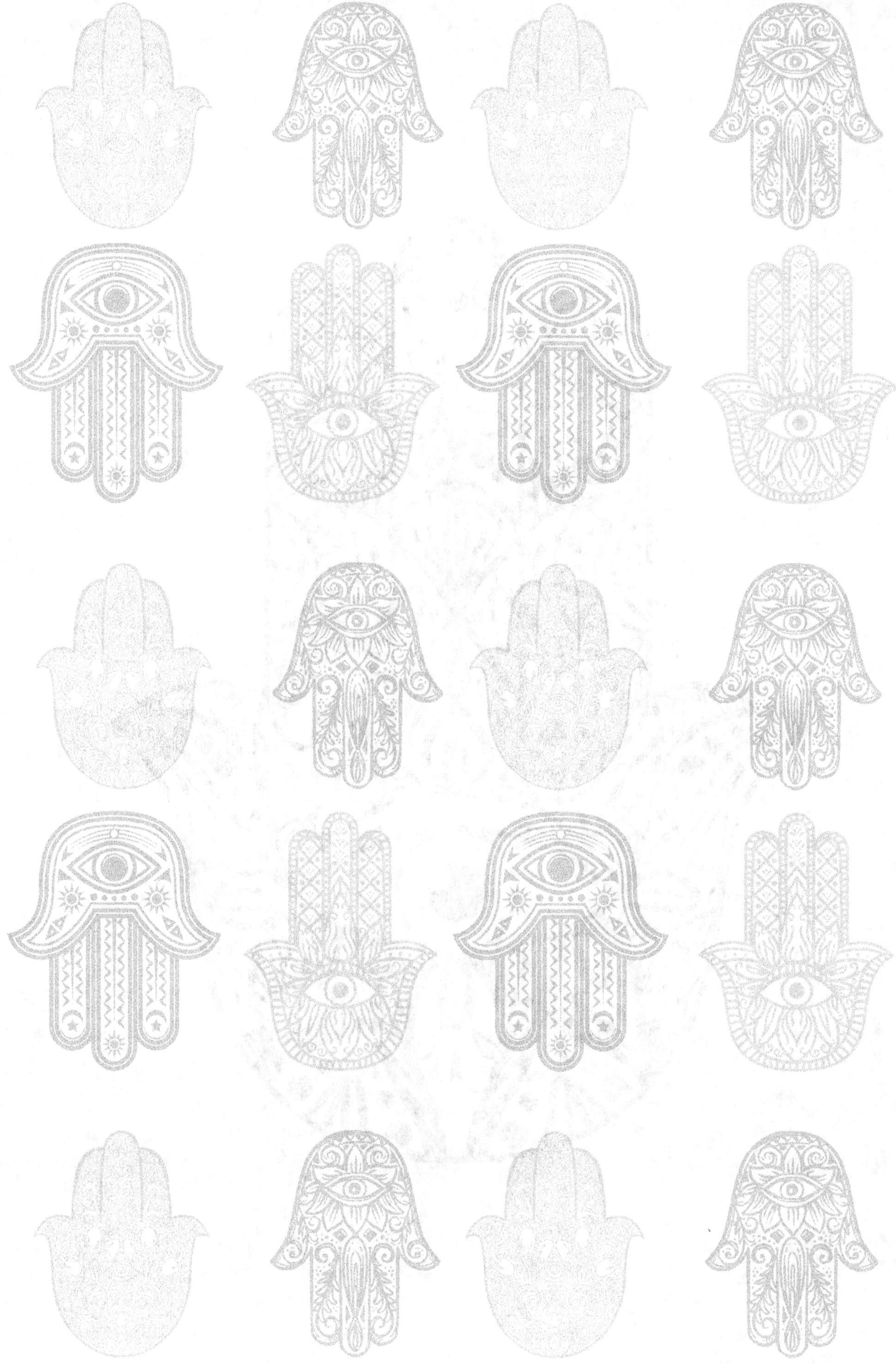

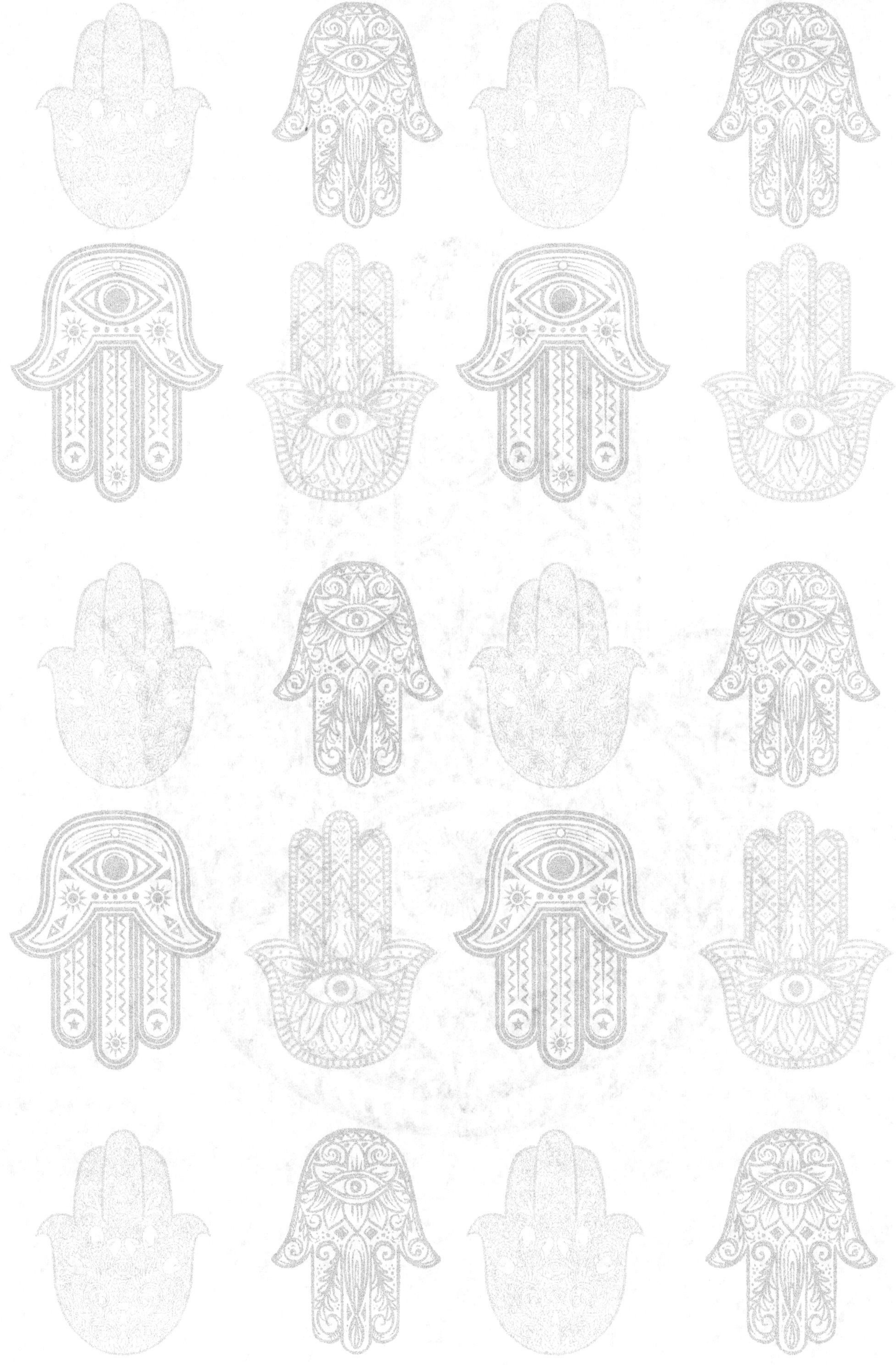

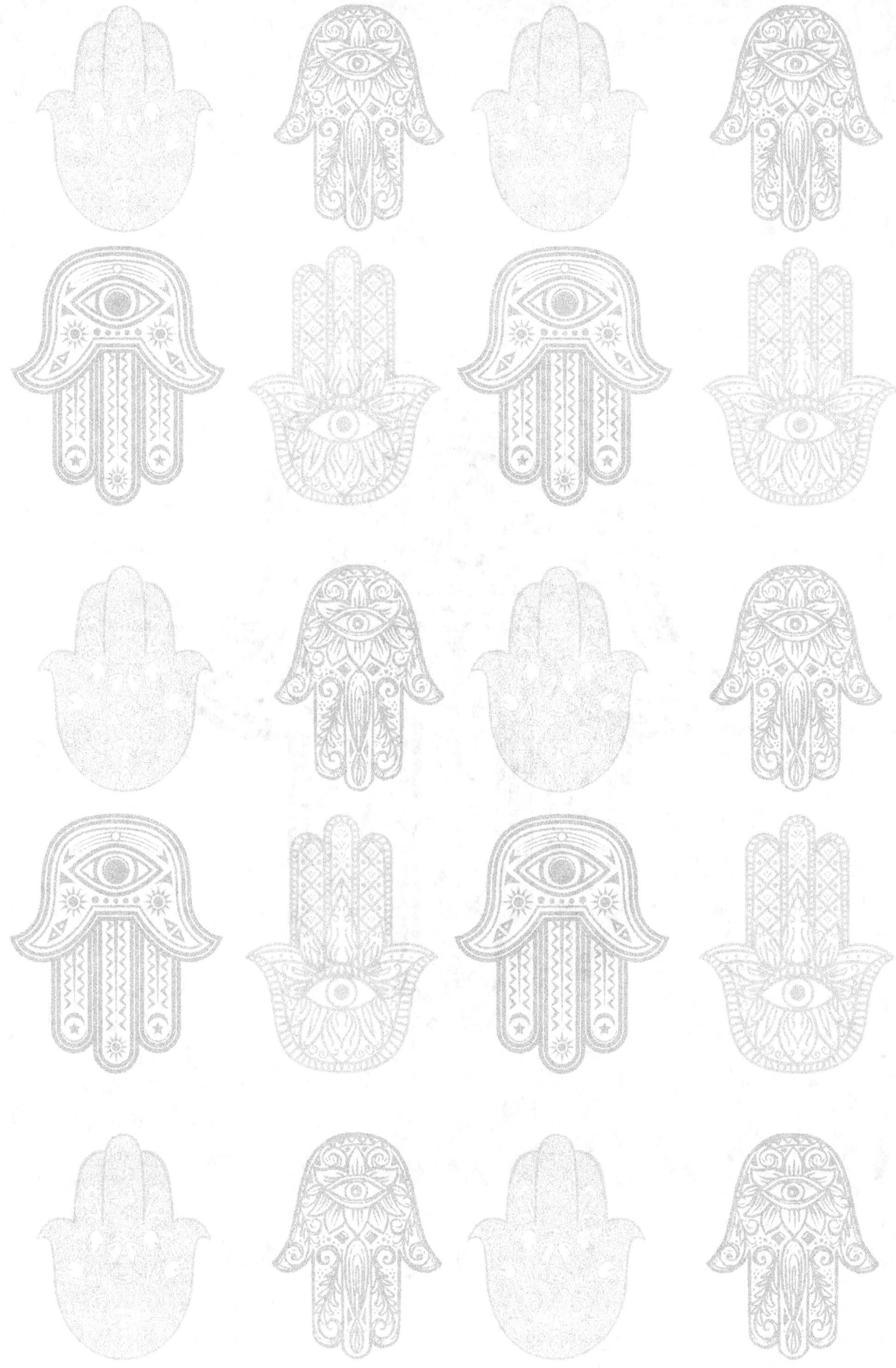

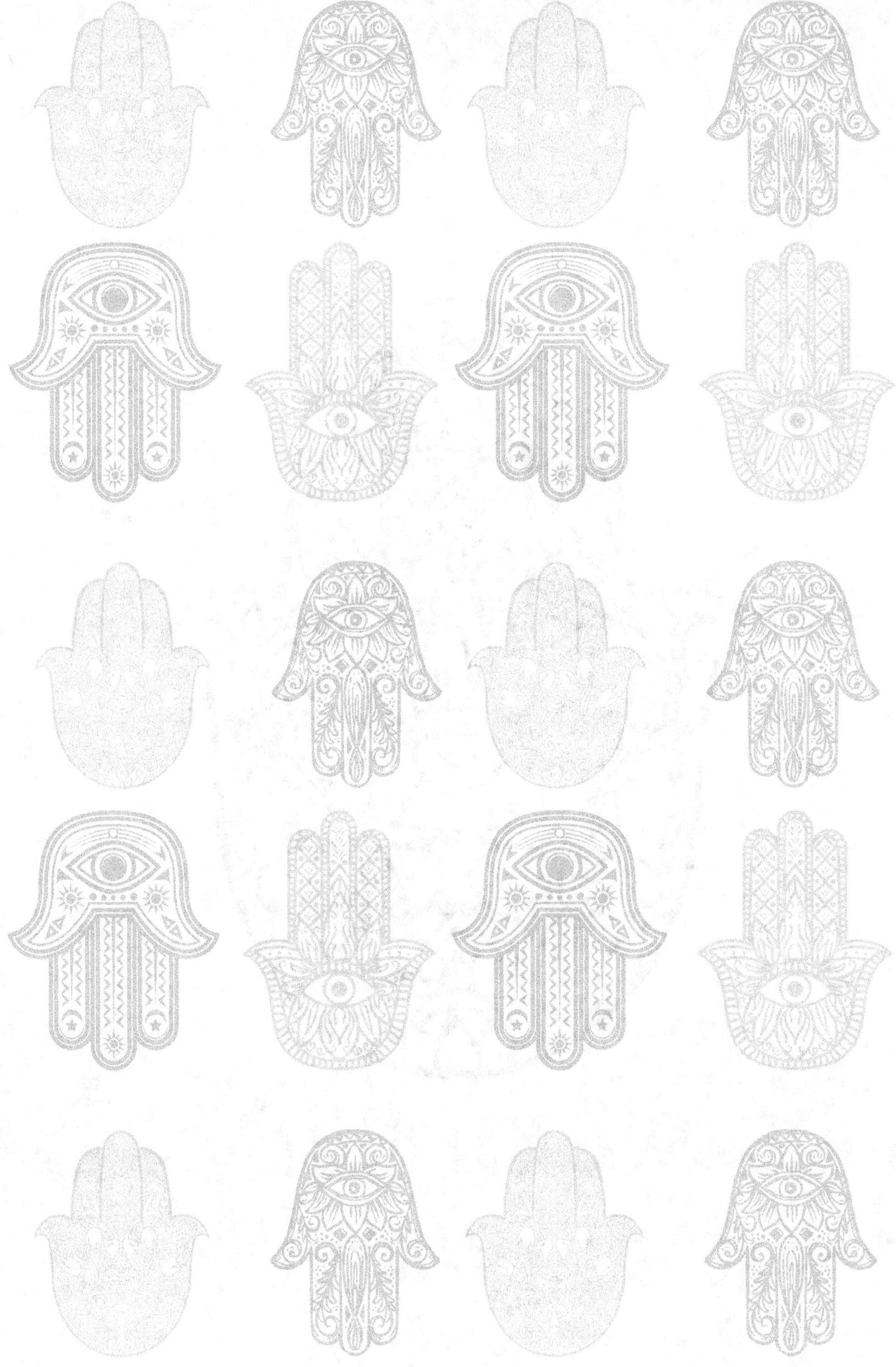

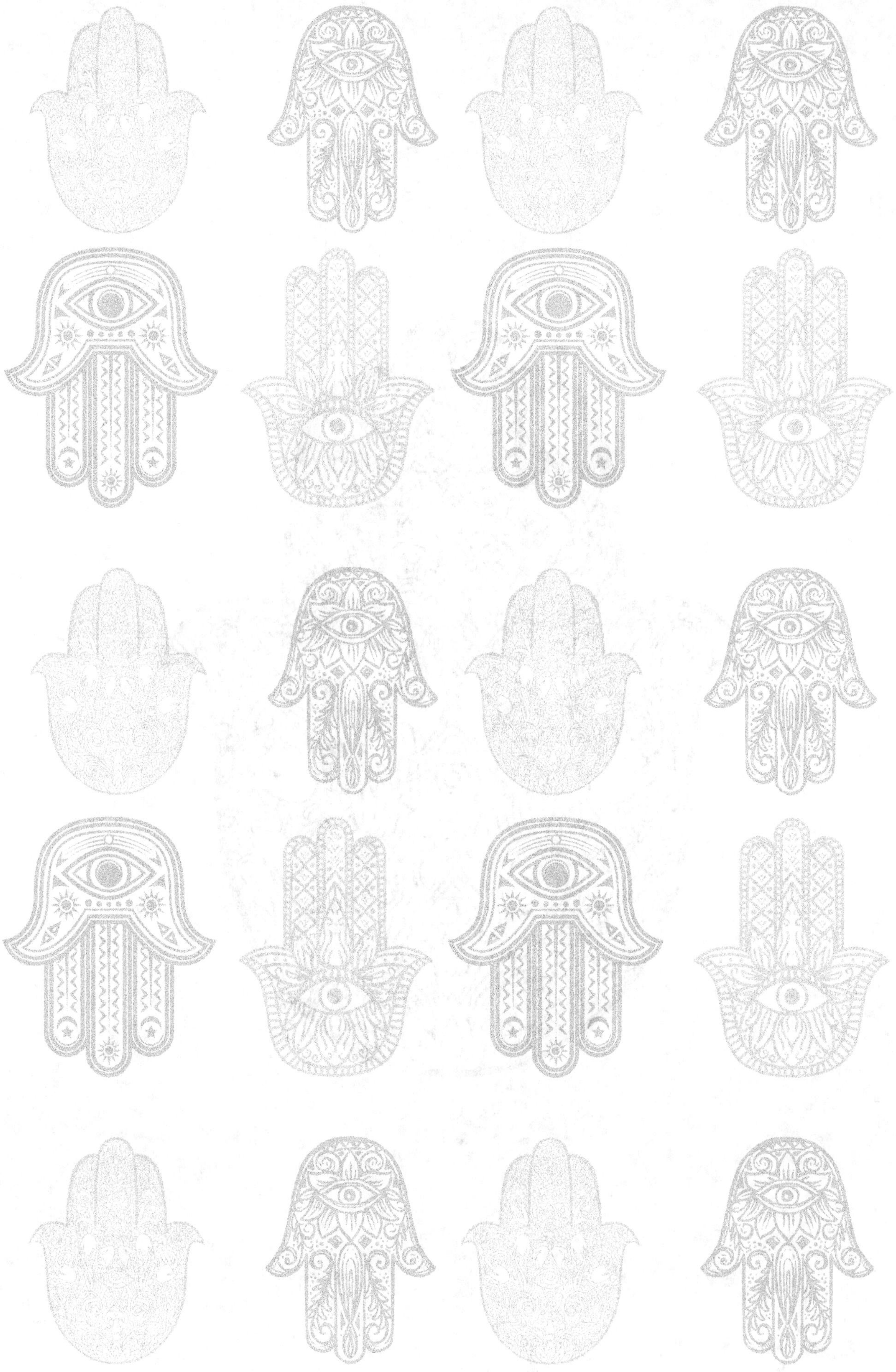

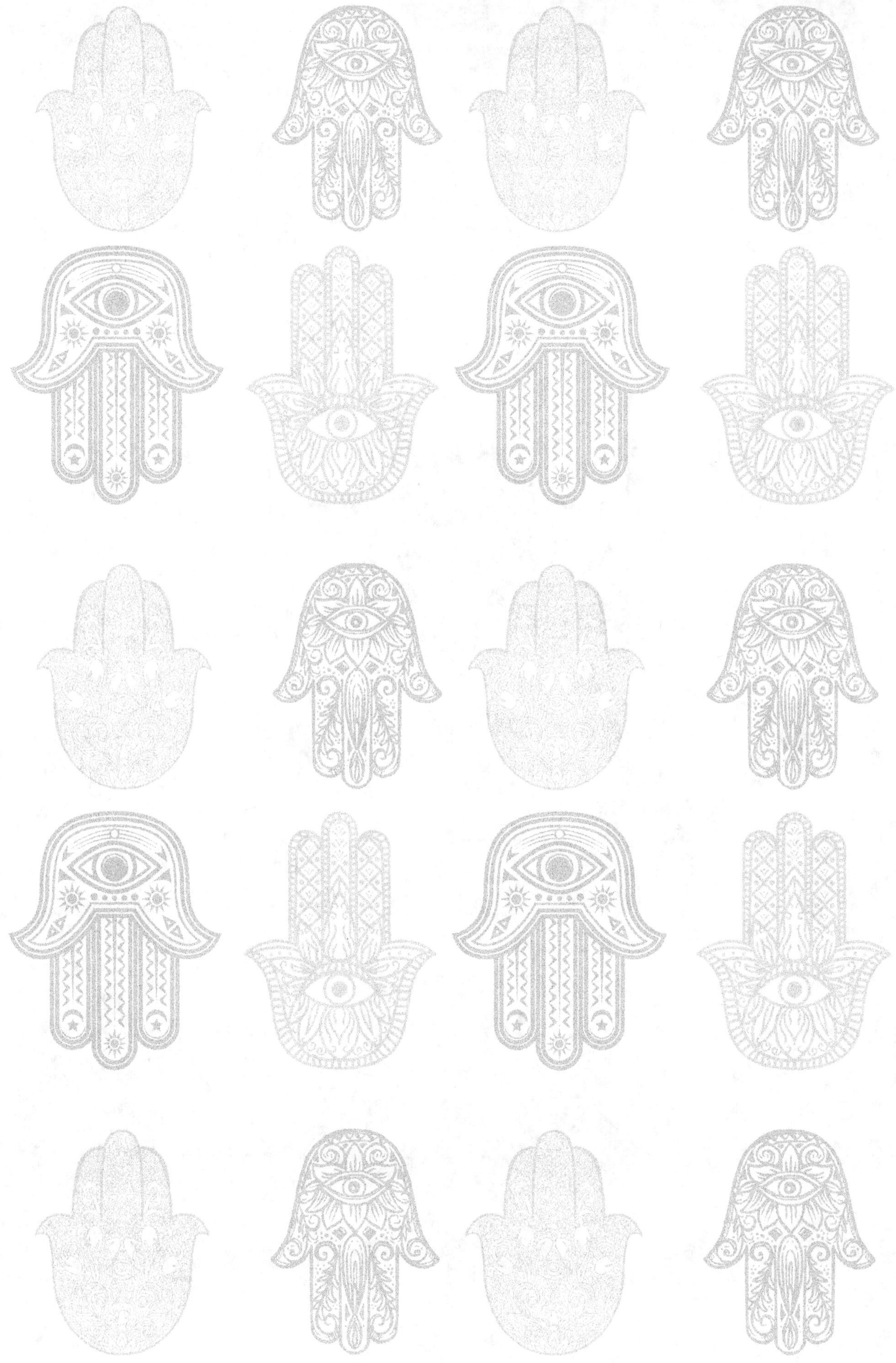

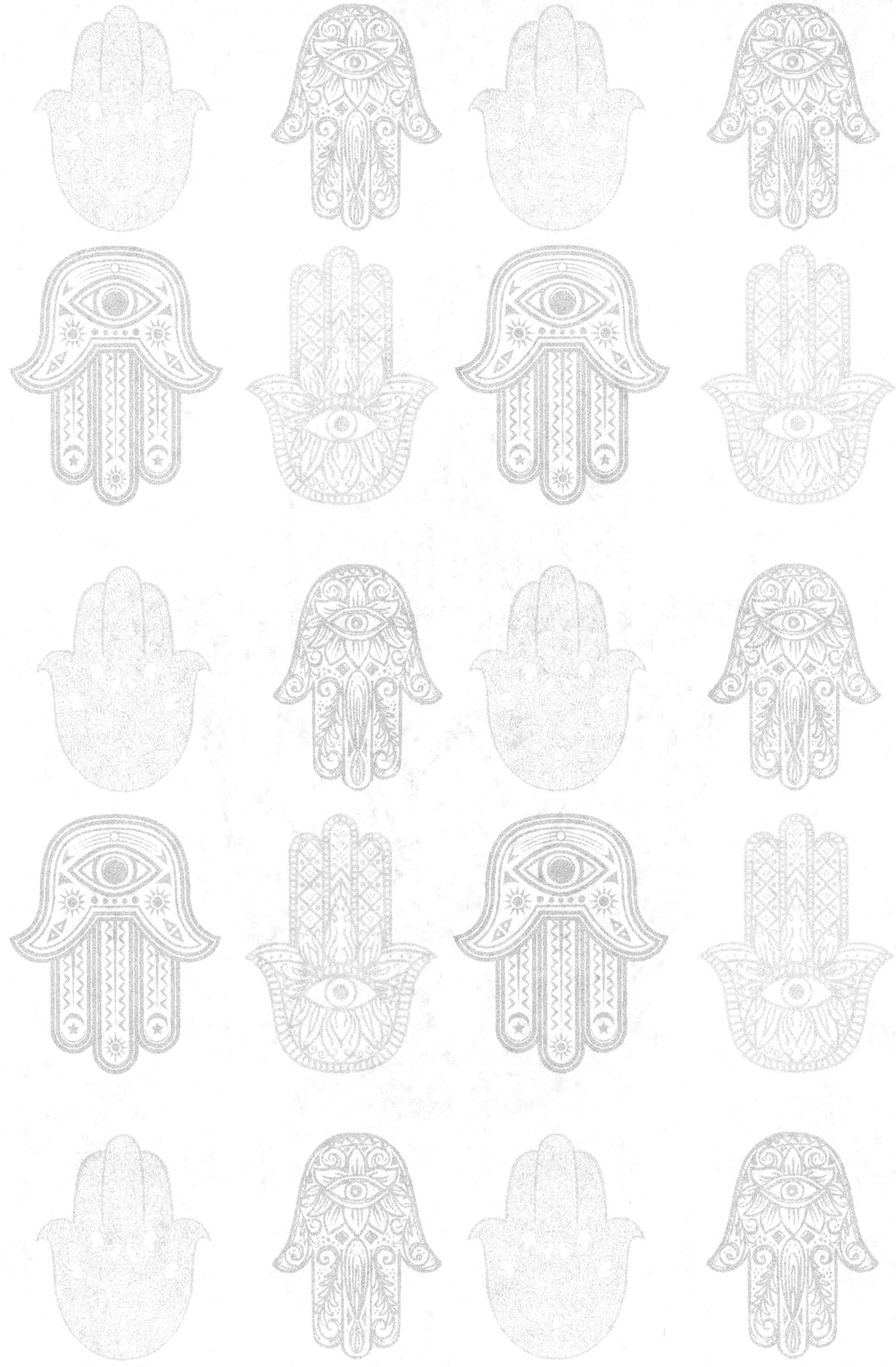

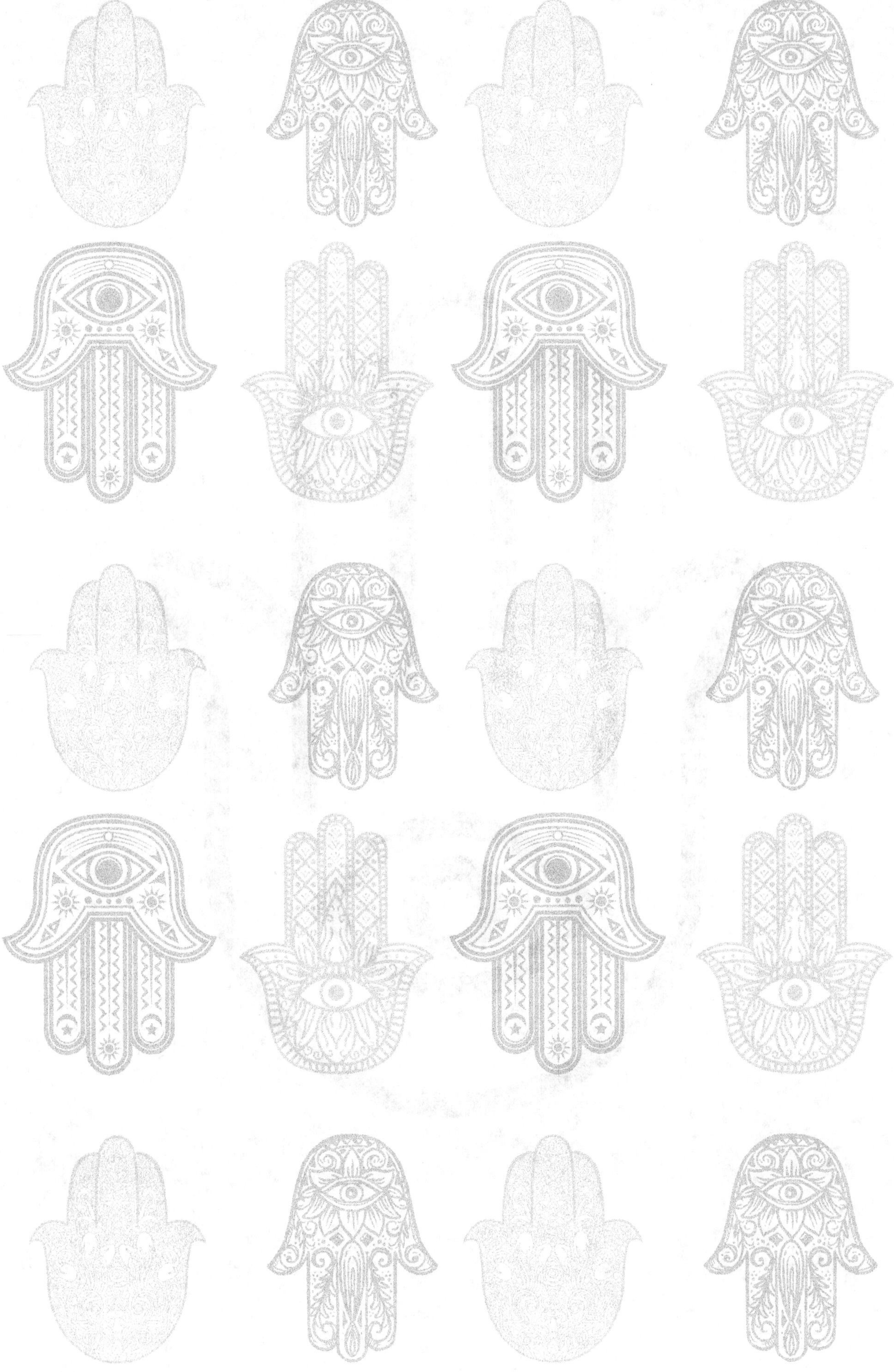

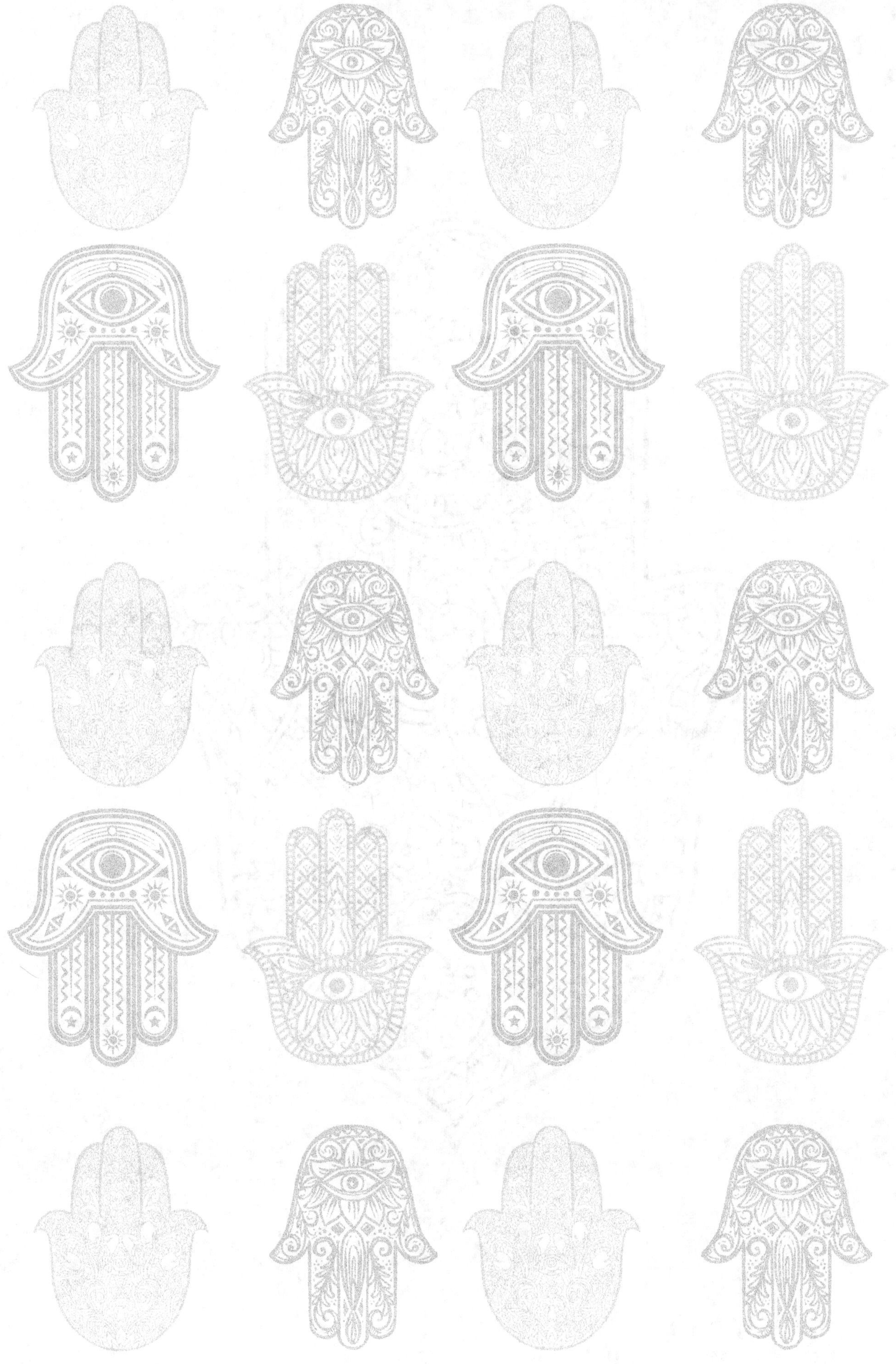

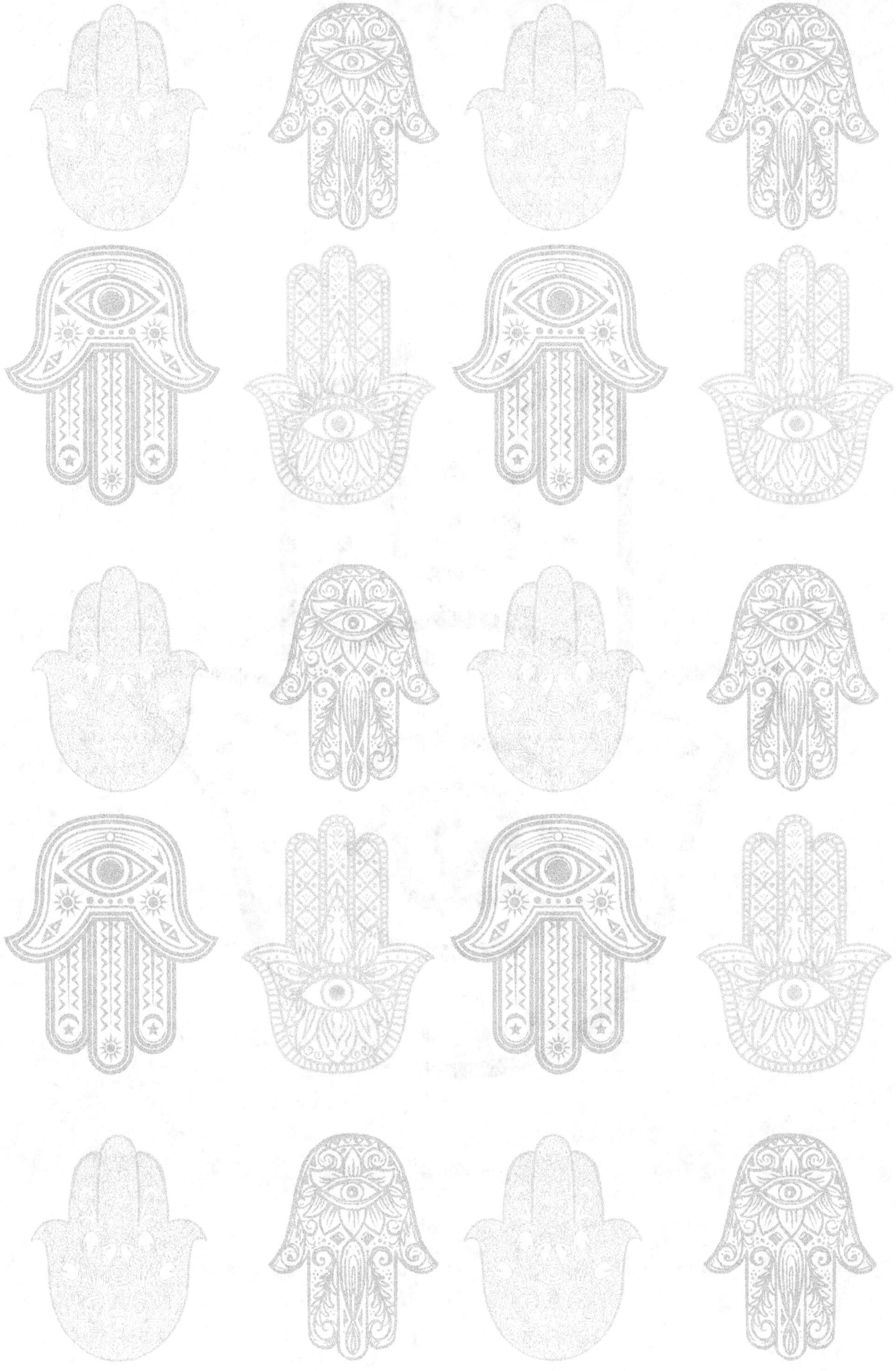

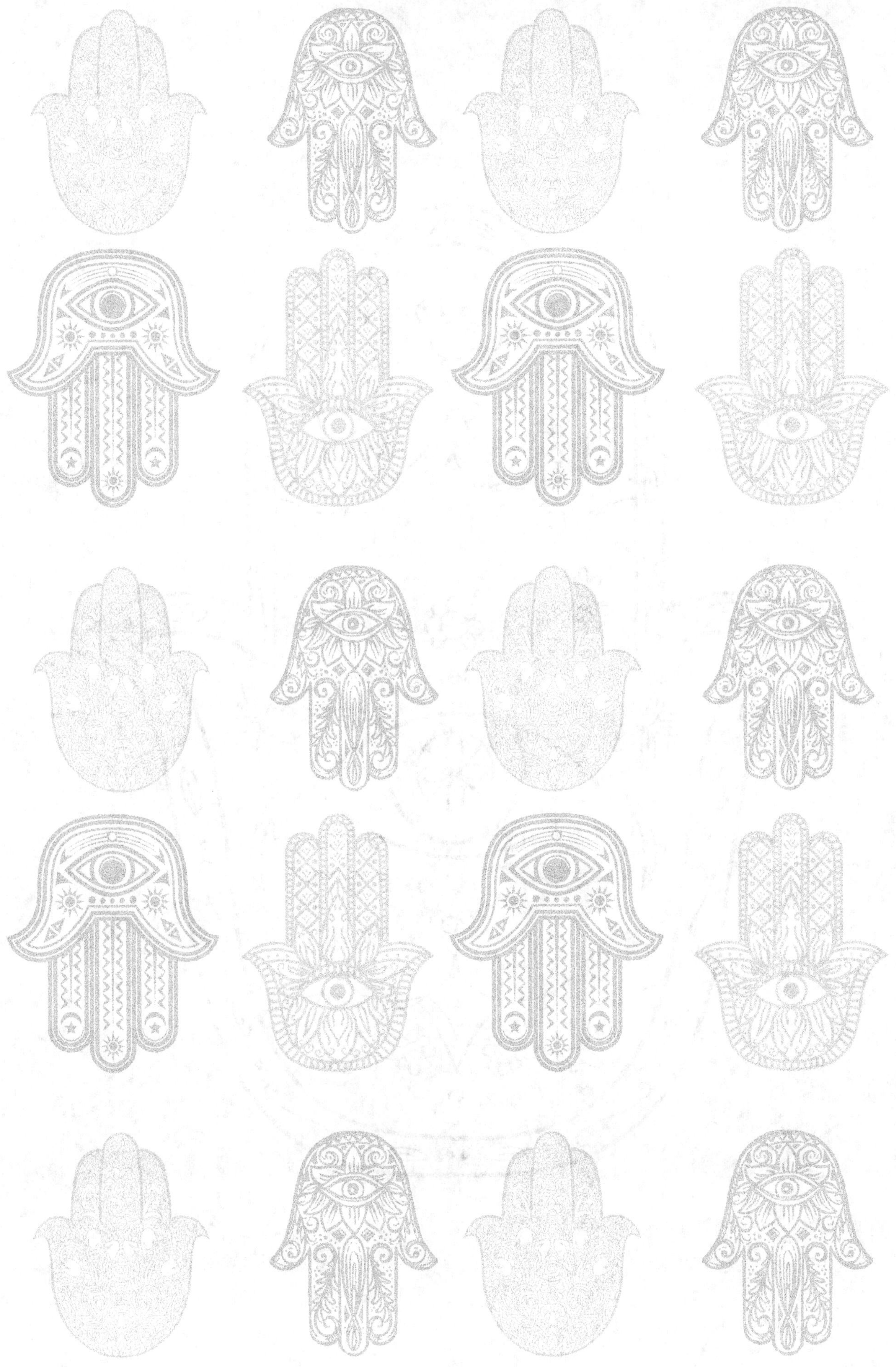

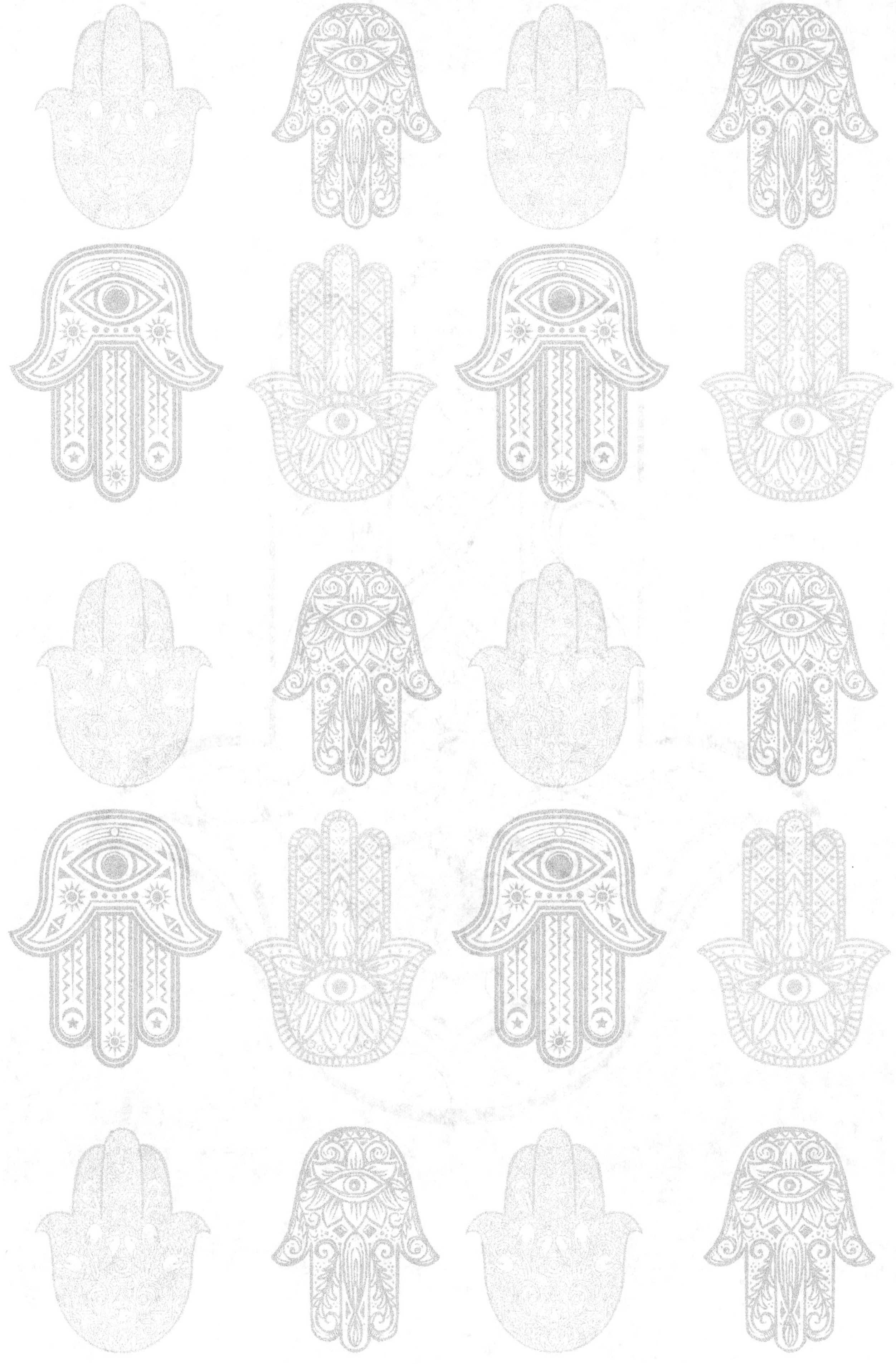

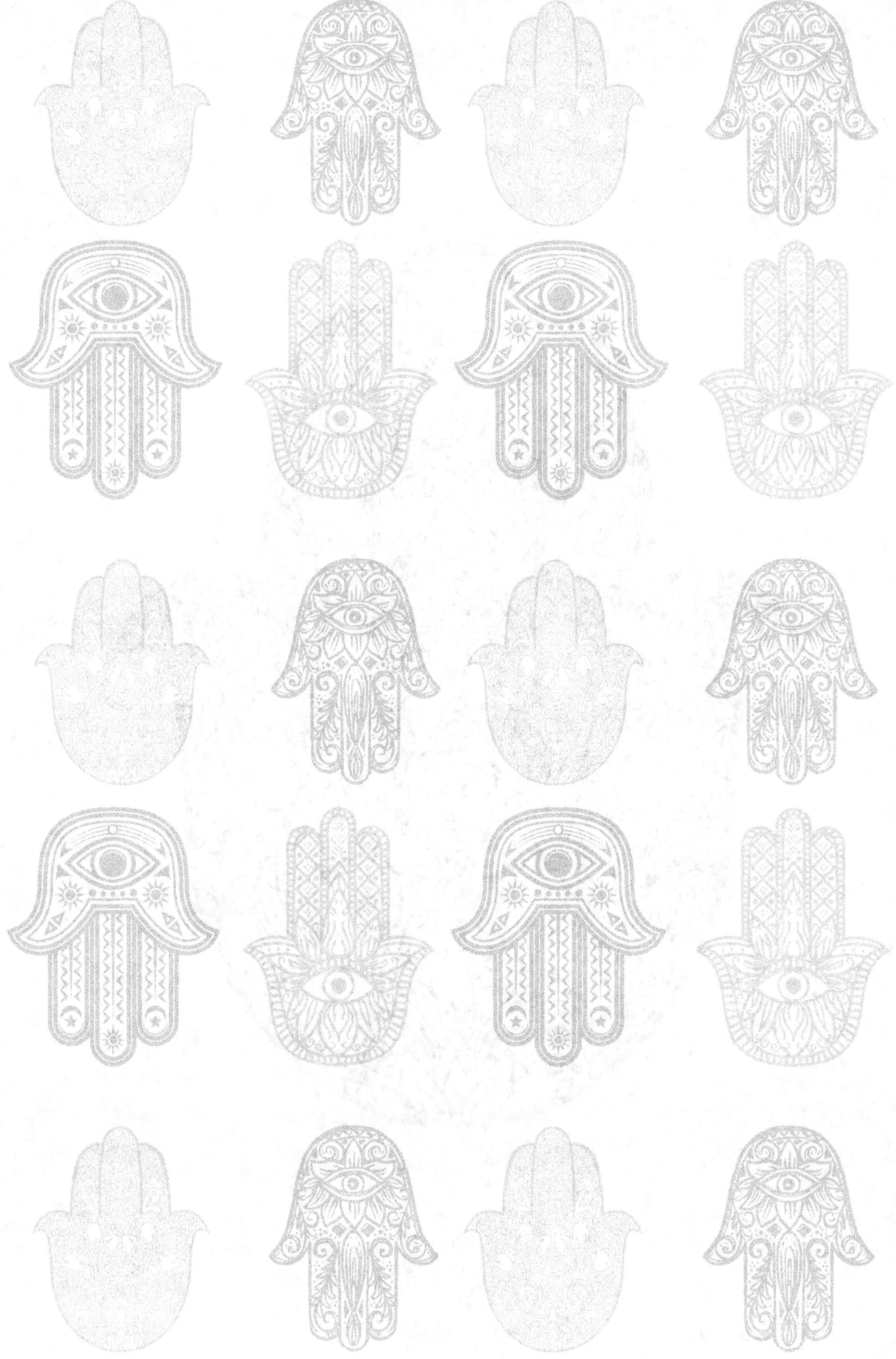

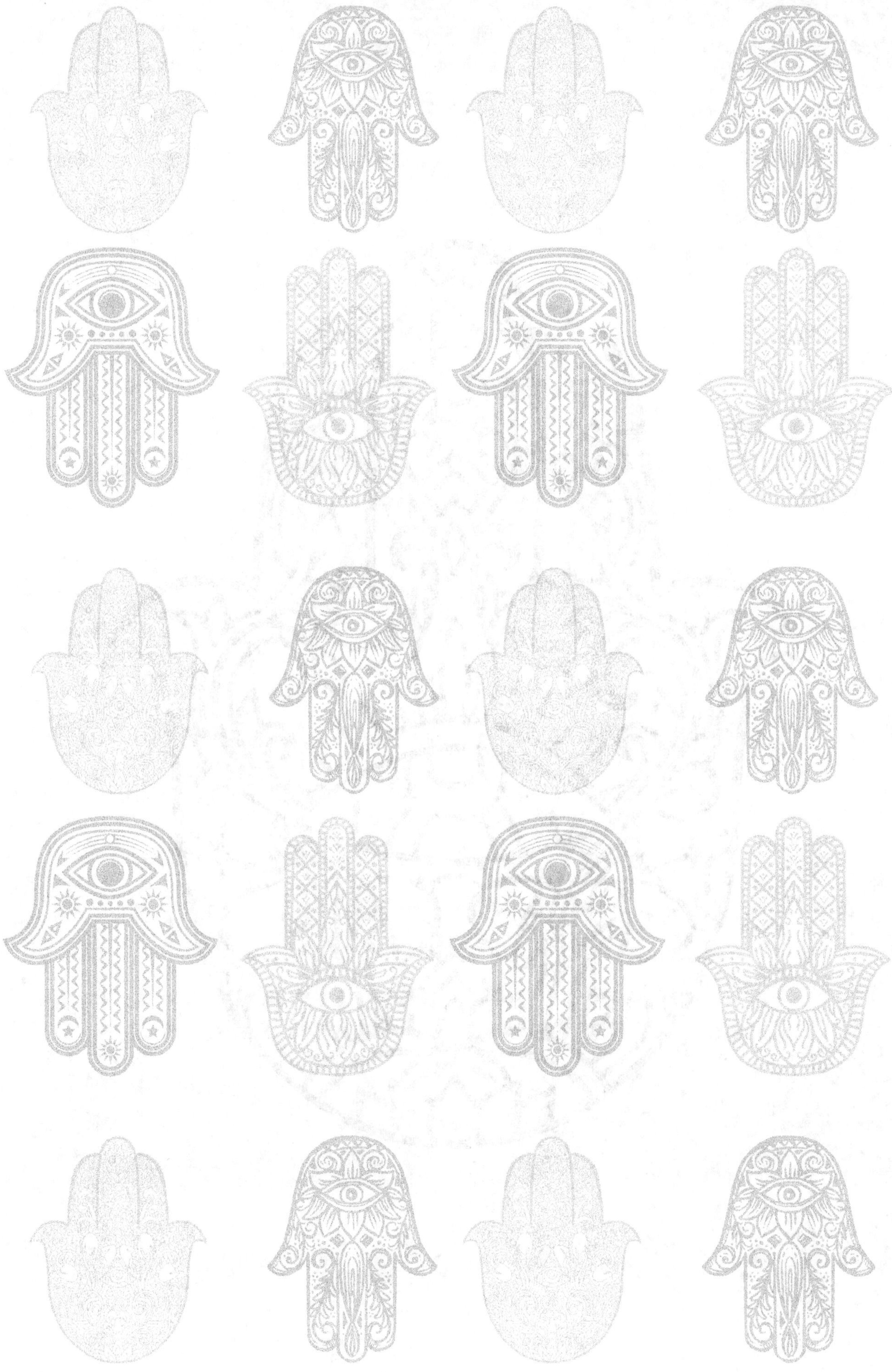

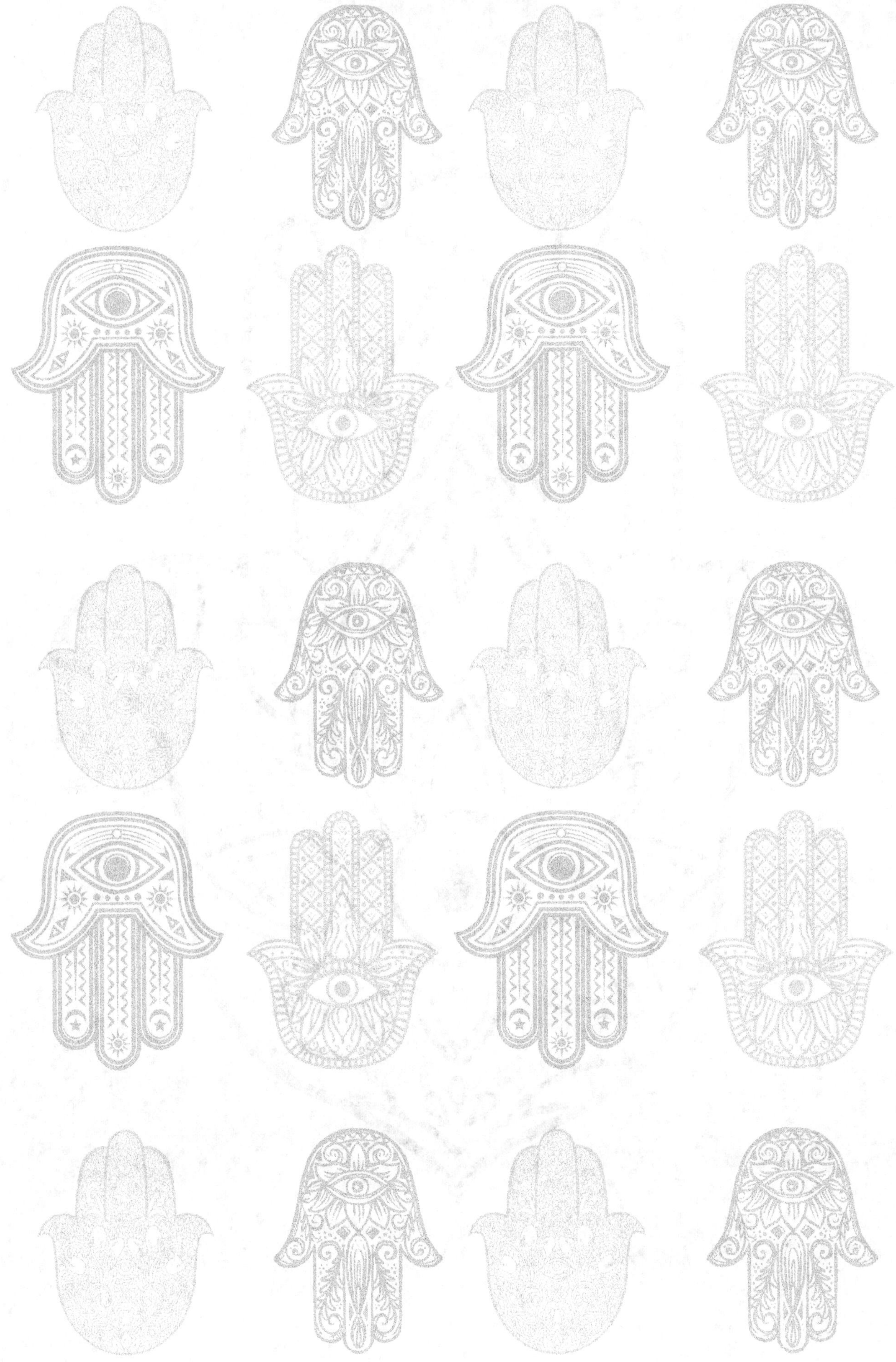

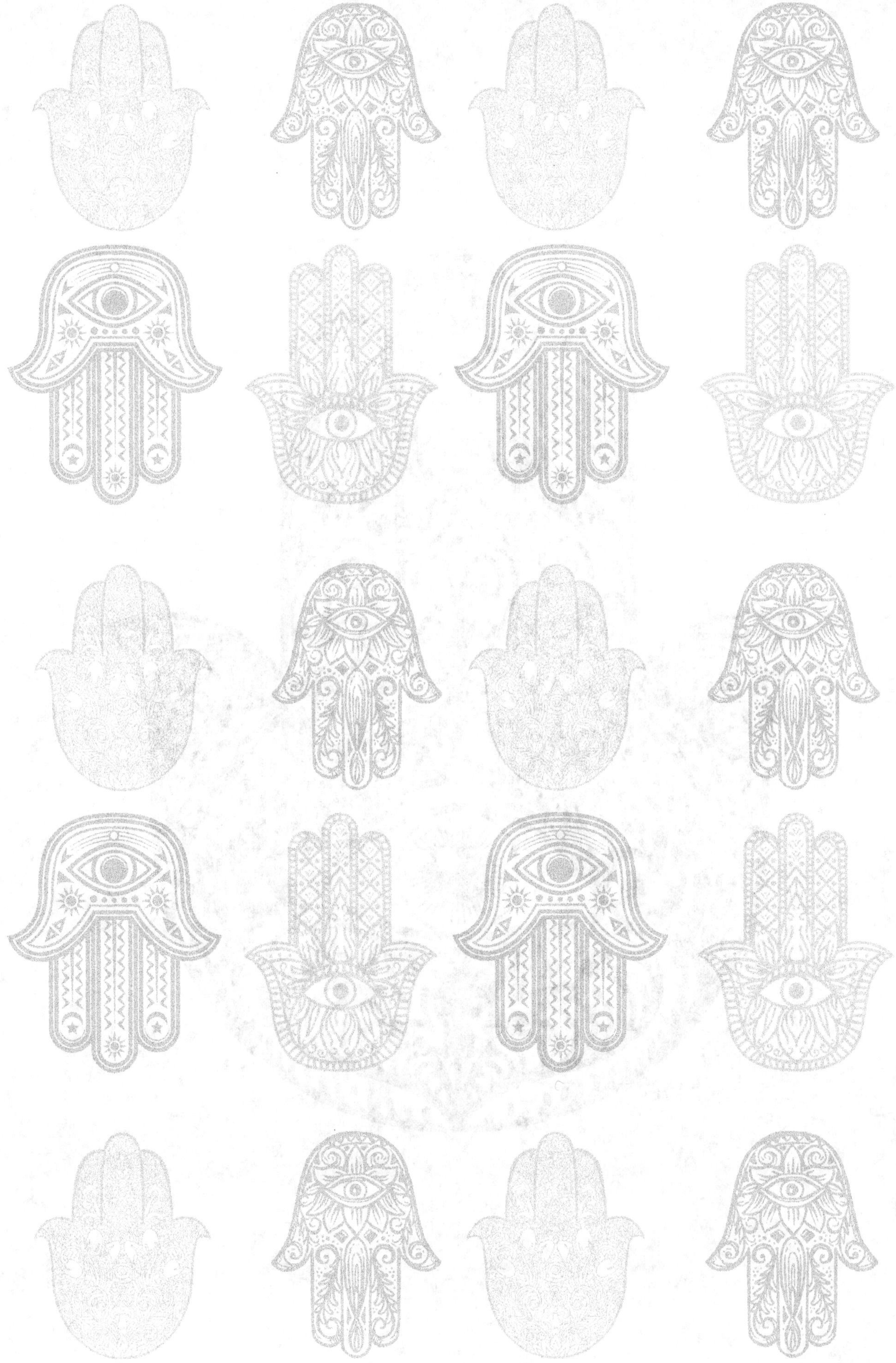

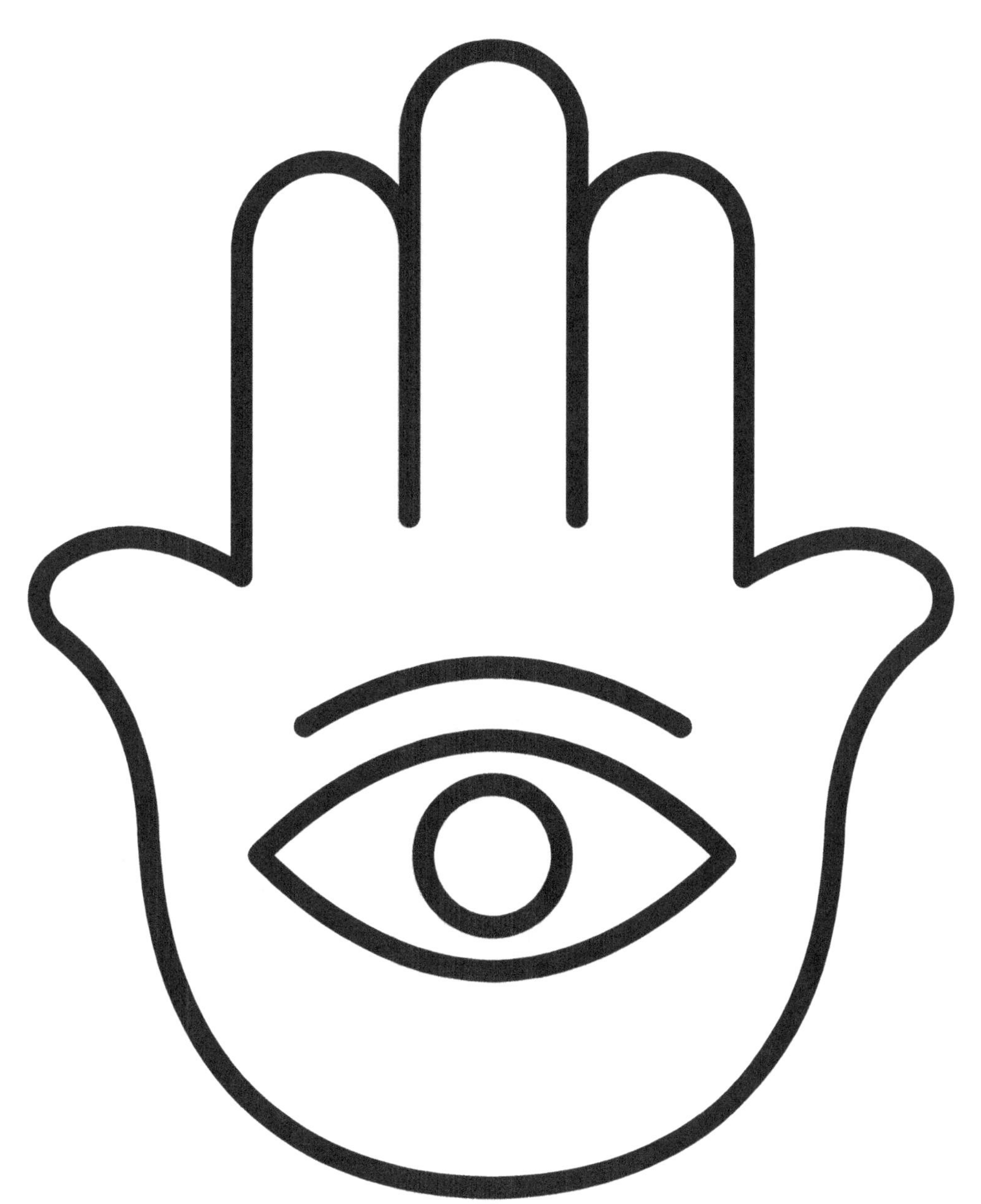

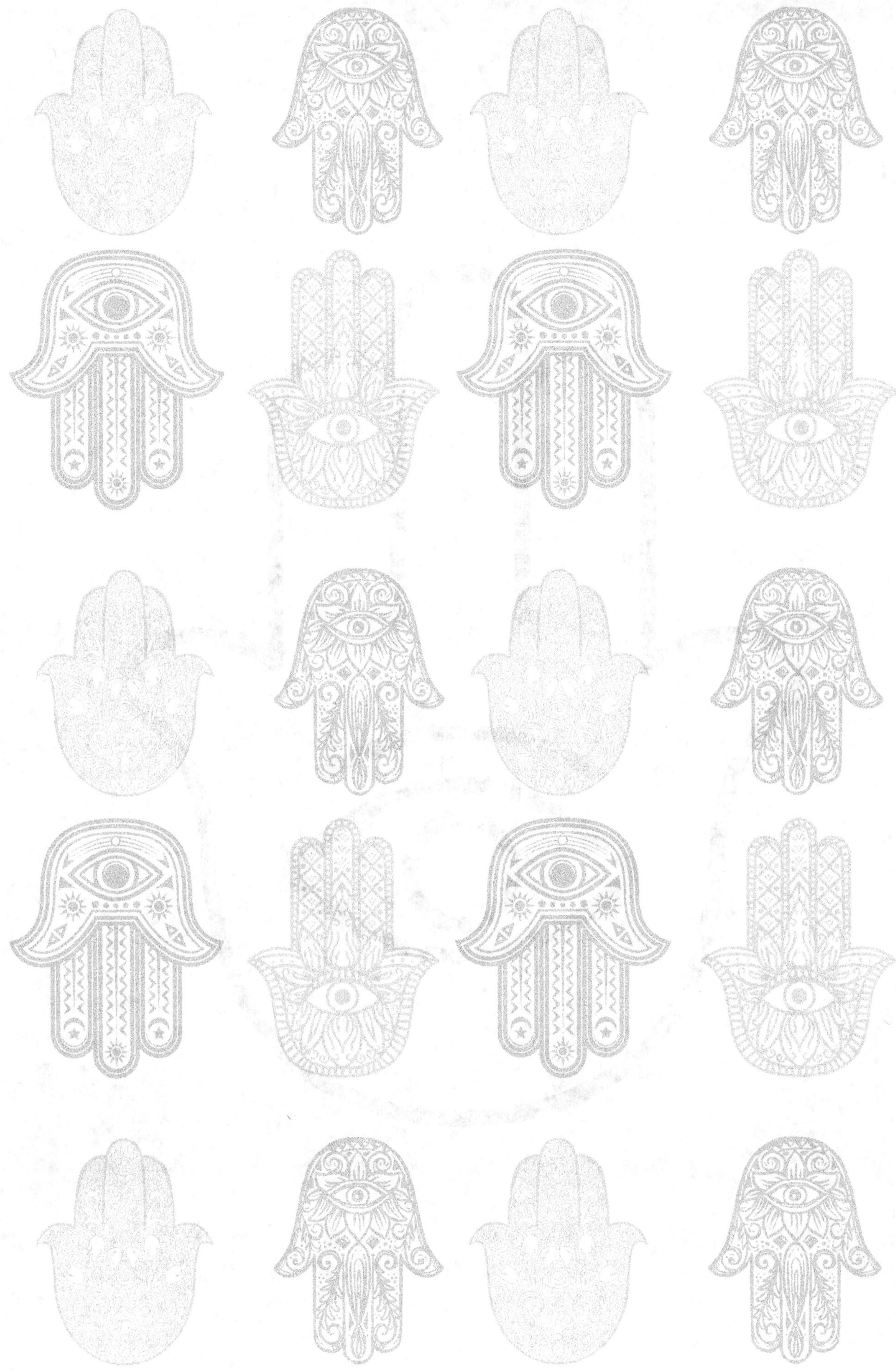

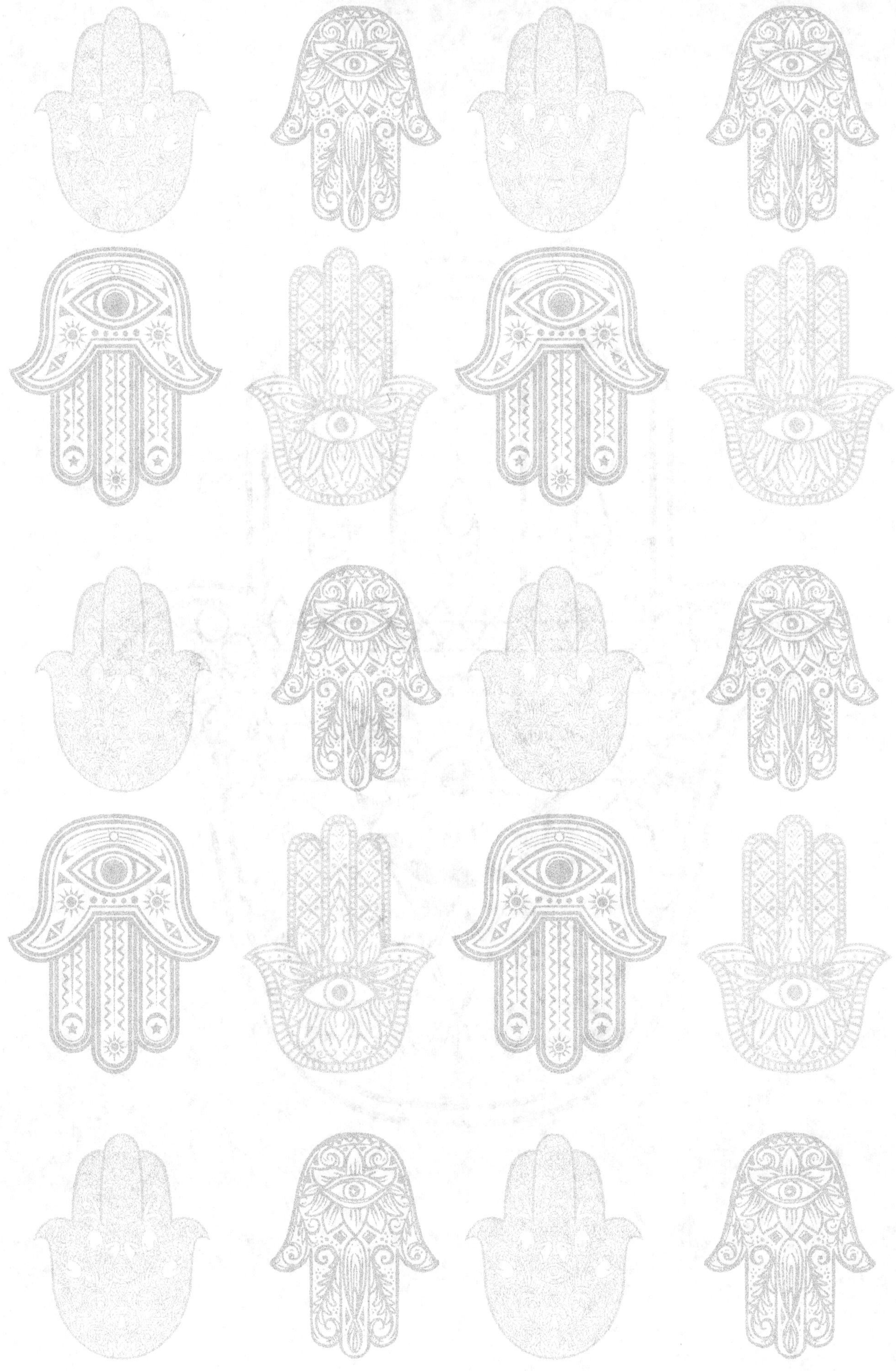

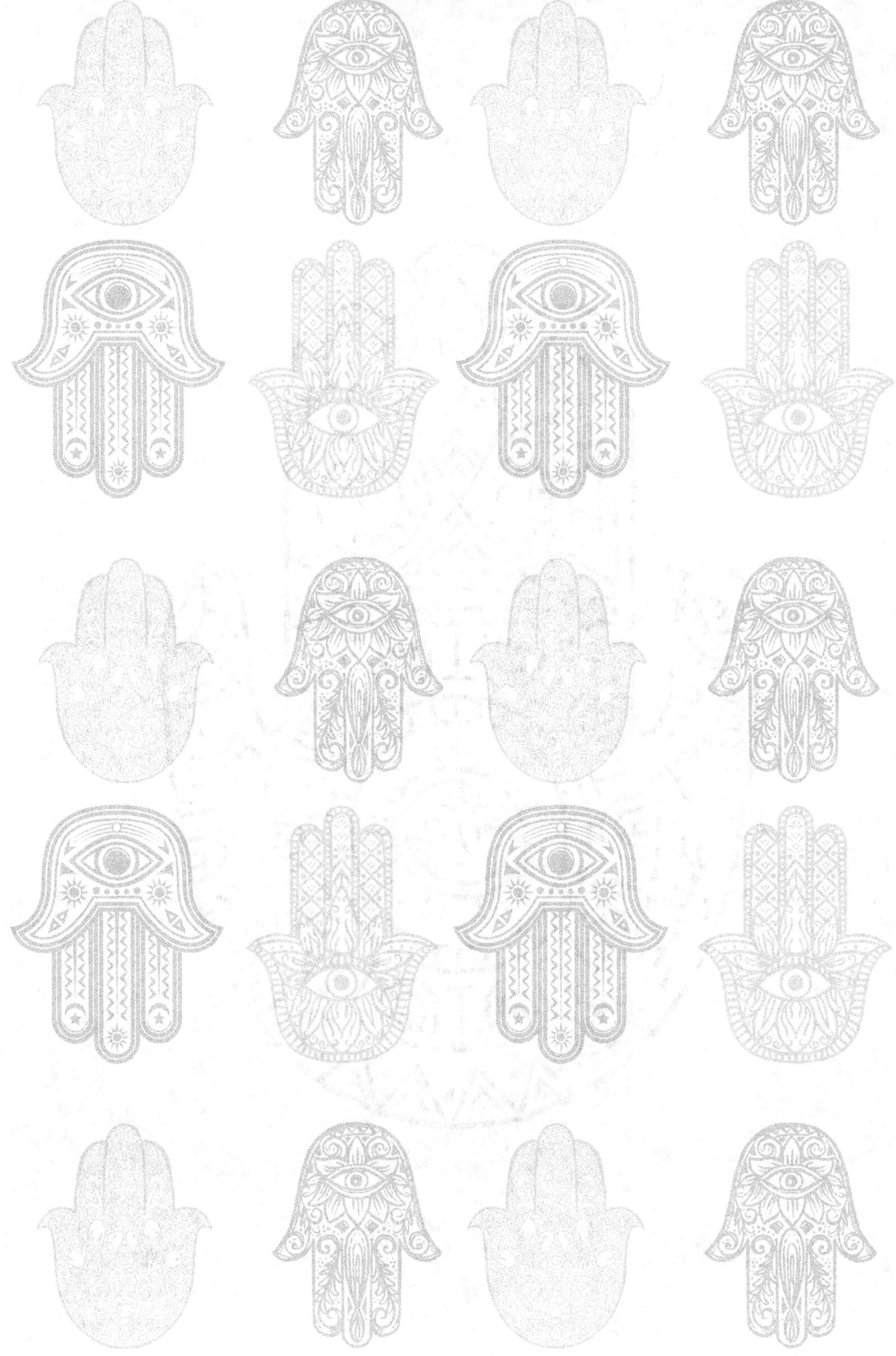

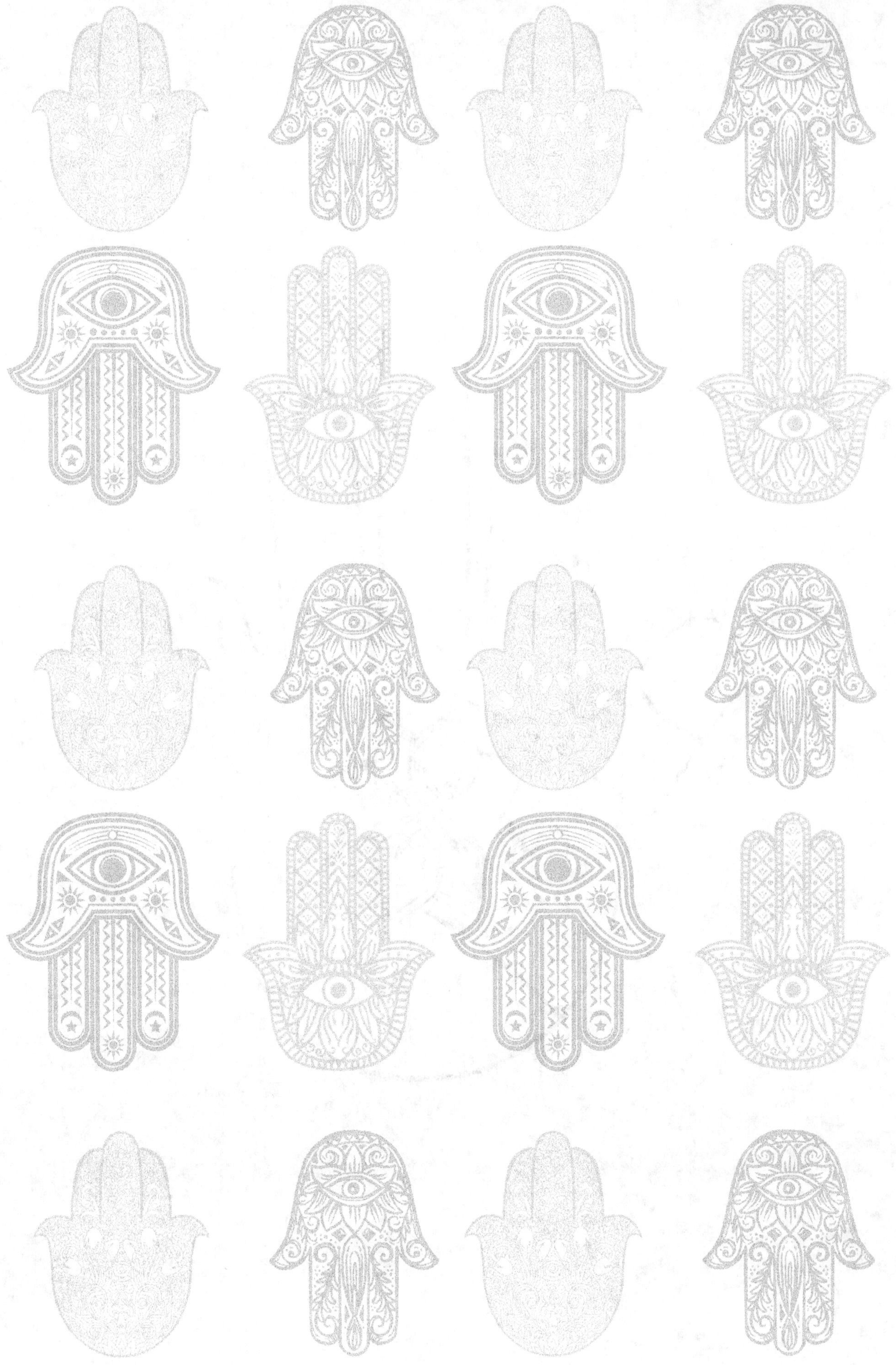

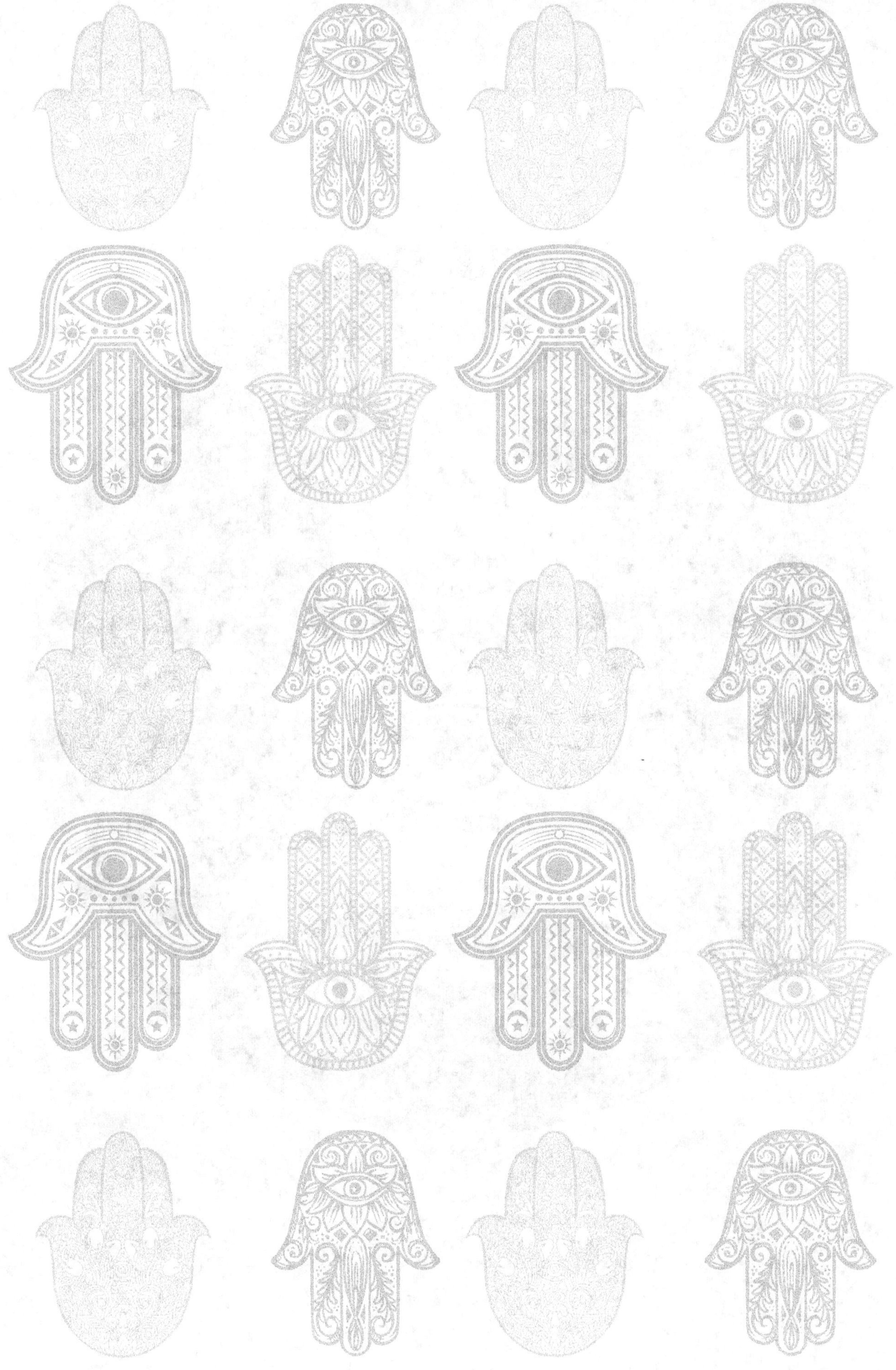

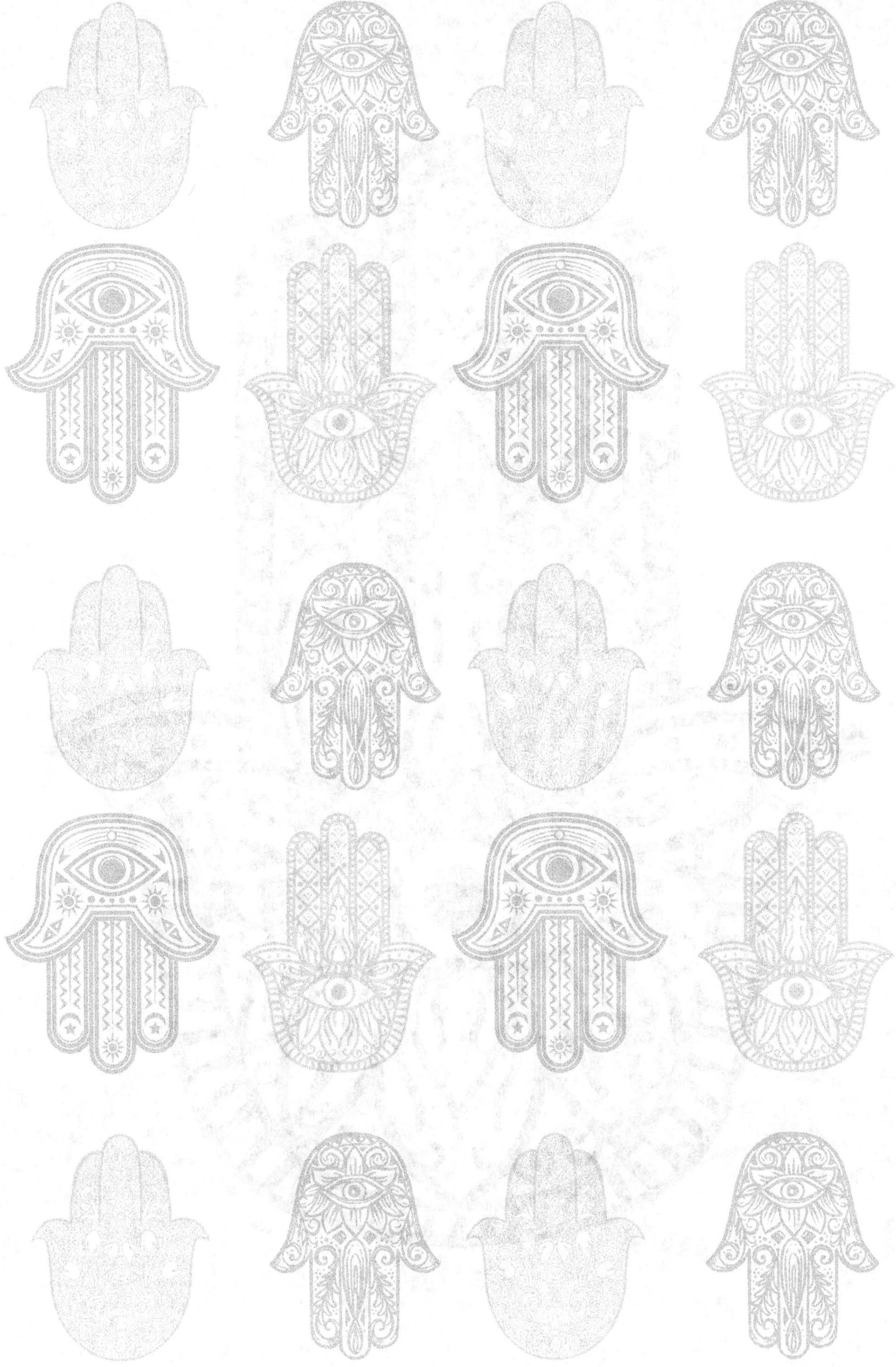

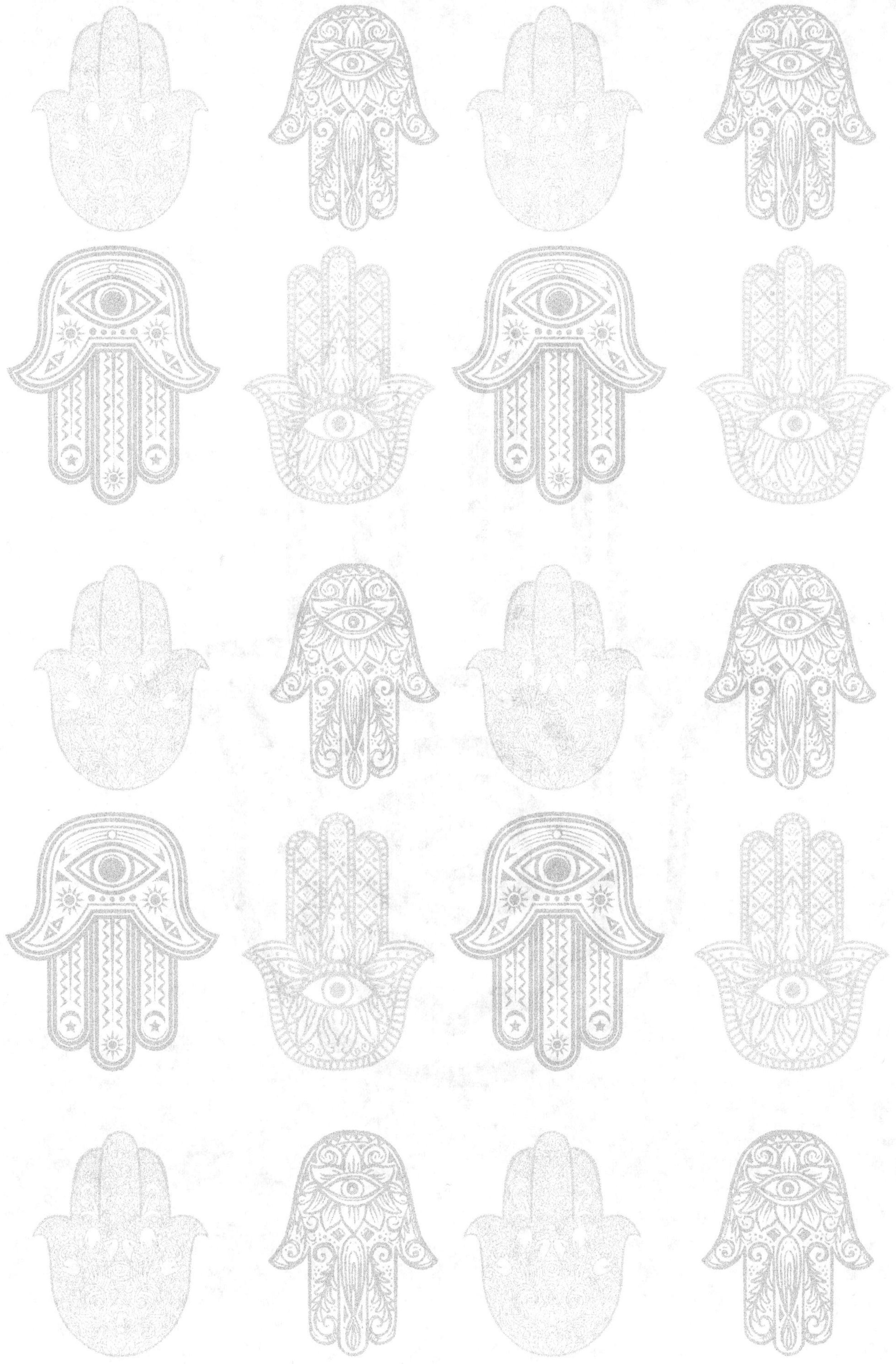

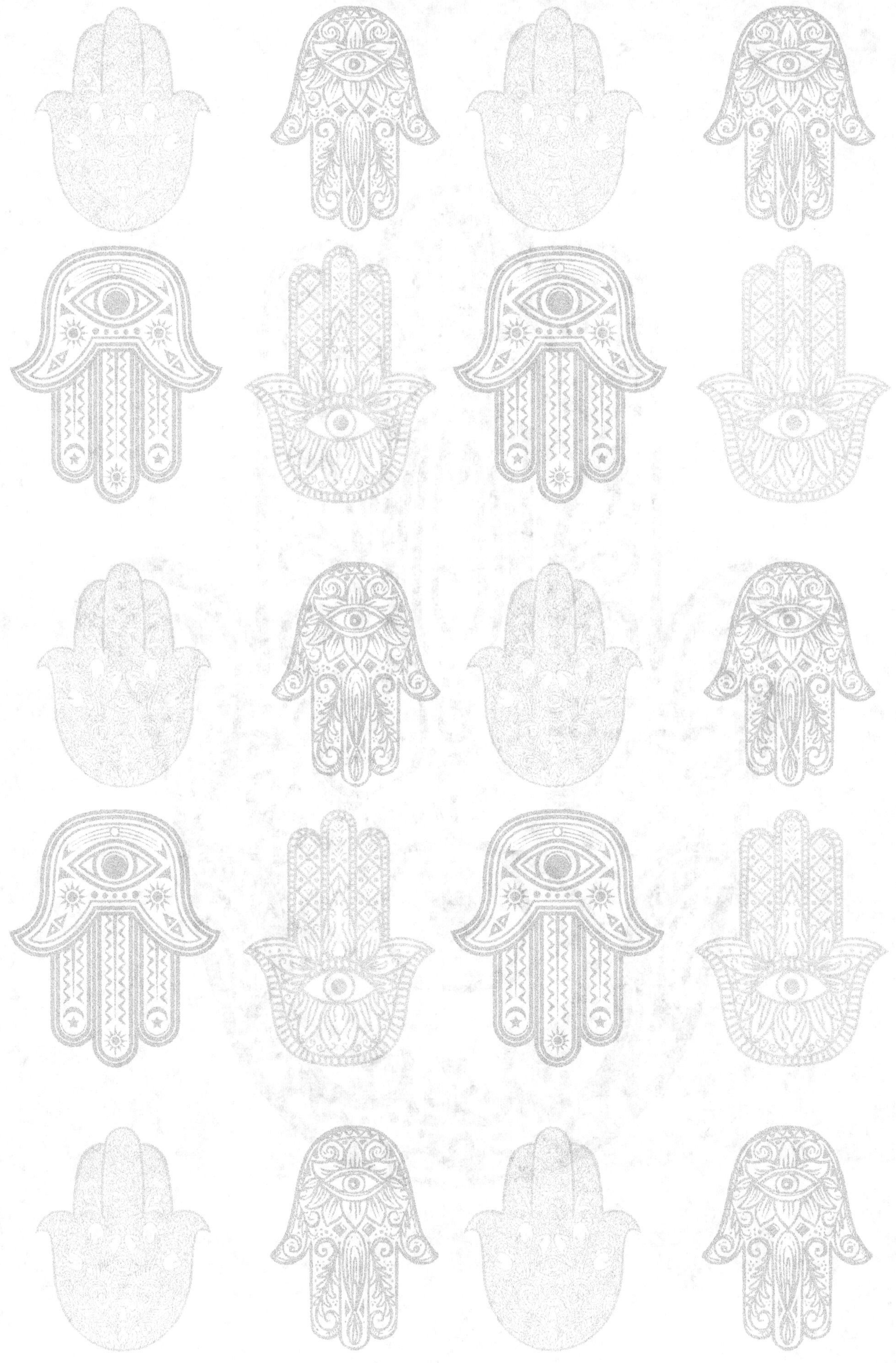

If you like this book, please give us a rate and tell us your opinion☺